CRYPTO BULL RUN INVESTMENT INSIGHTS 2025

BLOCKCHAINS BLUEPRINT ©

Foreword Dedication

To my cousins, family, and friends,

I dedicate this exploration to each of you. May this guide not only inform but also inspire you to think critically and embrace innovation in a time when digital currencies are shaping our financial landscape, I hope you find the knowledge within these pages empowering. Remember, the journey of learning offers not just insights but also invaluable lessons about the future of technology, finance, and our interconnected world.

May you always remain open to exploring the possibilities that lie ahead. With love and encouragement,

BLOCKCHAINS BLUEPRINT

Disclaimer

This book is intended solely for informational and educational purposes. The contents herein are not to be construed as financial, investment, legal, or tax advice. The author and publisher have made every effort to ensure that the information provided in this book is accurate and reliable; however, the complexities of the cryptocurrency market and the financial implications of investing in digital assets can vary widely.

Investment in cryptocurrencies and other digital assets carries inherent risks, and past performance does not indicate future results. The reader assumes full responsibility for their investment decisions.

The information contained in this book may not be suitable for all investors, and the author and publisher do not endorse any specific cryptocurrency, investment strategy, or financial product. By reading this book, you acknowledge that you understand the risks associated with investing in cryptocurrencies and agree that neither the author nor the publisher will be held liable for any losses or damages, direct or indirect, arising from your reliance on the information provided herein.

Furthermore, this book may discuss regulatory developments related to cryptocurrencies and digital assets; however, regulations are subject to change, and the reader should stay informed about applicable laws and regulations that may affect their investments. The author and publisher cannot guarantee the accuracy or completeness of information about future changes.

This book serves as a resource to enhance your understanding of cryptocurrency markets and related topics. Always conduct your due diligence before making financial or investment decisions.

Table of Contents

Chapter 1: Crypto Sectors

- Definition of Cryptocurrency Sectors
- Layer 1 Blockchains
- Real World Assets
- Gaming
- Artificial Intelligence

Chapter 2: Layer One Blockchains

- Bitcoin: The Pioneer of Cryptocurrencies
- Ethereum: The Transition to ETH 2.0
- Solana: Enhanced Transactions
- SUI: The New Chain in Town

Chapter 3: Rise of Real World Assets

- Physical Assets into the Digital Economy
- Opportunities for Investment
- Stability of Decentralized Finance
- Significant Partnerships in RWAs

Chapter 4: The Crypto Gaming Revolution

- Player Engagement through Blockchain
- Role of NFTs and Play-to-Earn Models
- Challenges and Opportunities in Gaming

Chapter 5: Decentralized Finance

- Eliminating Intermediaries
- Key Platforms in Decentralized Finance
- The Future of Finance

Chapter 6: Meme Coins: High Risk, High Reward

- Meme Coin Risks
- Highlighted Meme Coins

Chapter 7: AI Cryptocurrencies

- AI's Roles In the Crypto Universe
- The Use Cases and Different AI cryptos
- The Beginning of An Artificial World

Chapter 8: Pitfalls of Crypto Bull Markets

- Recognizing Market Psychology
- Risks of Leverage and Market Euphoria
- Regulatory Challenges & Market Volatility

Chapter 9: Tokenomics and Key Crypto Indicators

- Understanding Tokenomics
- Investigating Token Unlocks
- Assessing the Team and Development
- Evaluating the Website and User Experience
- Reviewing the Whitepaper
- Exploring Community Engagement
- Analyzing Market Position and Comparison

Chapter 10: Looking Ahead

- Macro Outlook
- Digital Money

Chapter 1: Crypto Sectors

Cryptocurrencies offer a decentralized alternative to traditional finance, decentralization means relying on an immutable global network of computers instead of bank ledgers. Crypto looks to increase the efficiency of the financial system while providing alternatives to traditional financial services. At the heart of this movement is blockchain technology, the backbone of cryptocurrencies. Think of blockchains as secure ledgers that everyone can see but no one can erase, creating a permanent record. Once a deal is logged in the blockchain, it's locked in like a vault, changing as practical as trying to turn back the tide.

Layer One blockchains are the foundations of the crypto ecosystem, picture them as the sturdy base of a towering skyscraper. The classic example is Bitcoin, introduced back in 2009 by the mysterious Satoshi Nakamoto. Bitcoin operates on a proof-of-work model where miners, or digital gold diggers use powerful computers to solve complex math problems that validate transactions and secure them on the blockchain. Other layer ones offer other consensus mechanisms like proof-of-stake and proof-of-history, all with their advantages and disadvantages.

Now step into asset tokenization to convert real world assets like houses, art, and commodities into digital tokens. Imagine being able to invest in part of a high-value property with fractional ownership, opening doors for everyday investors and democratizing wealth. Tokenization enhances access and ramps up liquidity turning assets into something that can be easily traded and shifted around the market.

Moving into the gaming world, cryptocurrencies and Non-Fungible Tokens are shaking it up big time. With games like Axie Infinity, players can own in-game assets they can trade, sell, or use elsewhere. Imagine earning real money while playing Super Mario, collecting coins instead of just racking up score points. It's akin to taking your passion for gaming and turning it into a profitable career, who wouldn't want that? This play-to-earn model is transforming casual gaming into a side hustle, blending fun and financial gain.

Decentralized Finance represents a revolutionary shift in how financial services are accessed and utilized. Think of decentralized finance as a vast fintech sandbox that removes traditional banking barriers. It allows anyone with an internet connection to lend, borrow, trade, and earn interest on their assets without the oversight of intermediaries. By using smart contracts decentralized apps automate these types of transactions transparently, securely, cheaply and without delay. This innovative approach empowers individuals with a level of accessibility and inclusivity that was previously unimaginable, where even the smallest investor can participate.

Meme coins have emerged as a fascinating and unpredictable segment of the cryptocurrency landscape, often driven by viral trends and online communities. Picture them as the playground of the crypto world, capturing attention with humorous origins, like Dogecoin, which started as a joke inspired by an internet meme. Meme coins have gained popularity and enjoy dramatic price fluctuations. The volatility and lack of underlying utility make meme coins a high risk gamble where the winners get rich and the market losers get stuck with the bag.

Adding a revolutionary dynamic is artificial intelligence. Moreover, AI is vital for maintaining security among many other use cases among which are artificial intelligence agents capable of completing a myriad of tasks at the click of a button. Artificial intelligence and blockchain intertwine in the crypto sphere to provide new abilities not previously known to man. This is the forefront of our future potential as a species, however, some say the human race should approach artificial intelligence with reprieve.

In a world where currencies are shifting from traditional to digital, understanding these key sectors is essential. The interplay among these sectors illustrates the continuous evolution of technology and its implications for investment opportunities. To capitalize on these opportunities investors must dive deeper into this chapter of technological advancement and financial inclusivity. Navigating this space requires not just technical savvy but also a keen awareness of the cultural shifts taking place. After all, the cryptocurrency revolution is a gateway to a more democratized financial future.

Chapter 2: Layer One Blockchains

When you think about the cryptocurrency movement it is impossible to ignore Bitcoin, the peer-to-peer electronic cash system that redefined global financial transactions. Bitcoin operates on a decentralized network known as blockchain where each block in this chain is like a page in a record book, secured through cryptographic methods. Bitcoin's proof-of-work mechanism rewards miners for their work in verifying transactions. This blockchain mechanism is known for significant energy consumption and the conversation around Bitcoin's environmental impact is more relevant now than ever. However, Layer 2 solutions like the Lightning Network reduce the energy consumption of the Bitcoin network by allowing transactions to be conducted off-chain, which minimizes the overall computational work and energy usage associated with each transaction processed on the Bitcoin blockchain. Other Layer 2 projects, like Stacks, allow users to earn interest on their Bitcoin without compromising the security or efficiency of the Bitcoin blockchain. Developments in the Bitcoin ecosystem will continue to expand and the utility of Bitcoin as a globally secure payment system will continue to be at the forefront of this financial evolution called cryptocurrency.

Beyond Bitcoin lies Ethereum, which has rapidly established itself as a decentralized finance platform. Launched in 2015, Ethereum transformed blockchain technology from simply being a ledger to a whole platform for building decentralized applications and executing smart contracts. It can be as easy as putting your money in and pushing a button, you can enter a binding agreement without needing a lawyer or other intermediary to write out contracts between two parties. That's the magic of Ethereum, as a base layer it can be used to build financial products that can connect users in trustless, immutable ways never before seen in traditional finance.

The upgrade to Ethereum 2.0, transitioning from proof-of-work to a more eco friendly proof-of-stake model reduces energy use while increasing transaction speeds and network capacity. Imagine a highway where cars no longer get stuck in traffic, zooming straight to their destinations. This transition will help Ethereum develop into the decentralized go to platform for smart contract applications. However, from an investment perspective Ethereum's old school reputation may not produce the returns one might see in newer projects depending on several factors discussed later in Chapters 8 and 9.

Next on the scene is Solana, a project that's been causing quite a stir. Its rapid transaction speeds and low costs are like the express train in the blockchain world, zooming ahead with a unique proof-of-history mechanism that allows thousands of transactions to be processed simultaneously. It's this kind of efficiency that developers require when building high performance decentralized applications. As Solana continues to grow, major partnerships with companies like Google Cloud and Mastercard are pushing its capabilities into mainstream finance. Solana, however, is most known for its non-fungible token markets more so than any of its finance applications, competing with Ethereum for the number two spot in crypto market caps.

Near is another blockchain worth mentioning as a developer-friendly blockchain tailored for the easy creation of decentralized applications. By incorporating innovative scalability solutions like sharding, Near offers low transaction fees and fast processing, encouraging developers to build within its ecosystem. Additionally, the vibrant Near community drives collaboration and project development, positioning the platform to be a significant player in the blockchain space as it evolves alongside growing decentralized finance solutions.

Layer One blockchains serve as the foundational networks that provide the essential infrastructure for executing transactions and smart contracts and as the blockchain ecosystem expands, the need for interoperability between blockchains becomes increasingly crucial. This is where Chainlink and Axelar come into play. Chainlink connects blockchains to real-world data through its decentralized oracle network, enabling smart contracts to access off-chain information securely. Meanwhile, Axelar facilitates seamless cross-chain communication, allowing different blockchains to interact and exchange assets or data. Together, Chainlink and Axelar enhance the functionality of Layer One solutions, enabling a more interconnected and efficient blockchain ecosystem that can accommodate diverse applications and user needs.

Chainlink serves to bridge the gap between blockchains, applications, and the external environment. Its wide adoption across decentralized protocols highlights the increasing need for real-time data making Chainlink a pivotal component in advancing the functionality of smart contracts. It has been working closely with the banking sector to facilitate smoother bank to bank transactions using its Cross-Chain Interoperability Protocol. CCIP enables smart contracts on one blockchain to access external data and execute transactions across various chains, effectively bridging the gap between decentralized finance and traditional finance. By enhancing interoperability, CCIP allows for a more seamless integration of blockchain technology into the existing financial infrastructure.

Axelar stands out for its cross-chain communication capabilities also, enabling seamless interactions across multiple blockchains. By offering developer tools for building cross-chain applications, Axelar is promoting interoperability and scalability in a landscape where fragmentation poses challenges. This focus not only enhances user experience but also encourages broader adoption of blockchain technologies, making Axelar a notable player in the quest for a more interconnected crypto ecosystem.

In summary, the realms of Bitcoin, Ethereum, Solana, Near, and emerging cross-chain communication collectively illustrate a transformative journey where finance meets technology, ushering in a new era of economic potential where understanding these pivotal components is key to navigating the fast-paced world of cryptocurrency.

Chapter 3: Rise of Real World Assets

In the cryptocurrency sphere we are witnessing the rise of 'real world assets'. Imagine having the ability to merge physical assets, like real estate and commodities, with the digital world of blockchain. The added benefit of instant liquidity and accessibility to asset classes allows for connectivity in the new age of finance opening up endless potential for new asset pairs..

Real world assets are tangible assets converted into tokens and accessible on blockchain platforms. By addressing traditional barriers tokenization enhances liquidity and opens the door for a broader range of investors, think of it as turning a brick-and-mortar store into an online marketplace where shopping becomes easier for everyone. By allowing fractional ownership, people can own a piece of high value investments that were previously out of reach, leveling the playing field for everyday investors.

Take real estate as a prime example. Historically, real estate investments required significant capital upfront, often leaving small investors sidelined. Now, through tokenization, investors can buy fractions of a property as tokenized shares, thus democratizing access to the real estate market. This shift is similar to how crowdfunding has changed the way we support projects, everyone can now participate.

Picture trying to build a house with sand instead of bricks, the structure is bound to crumble. One of the biggest challenges in decentralized finance has been the reliance on volatile cryptocurrencies as collateral. Incorporating real world assets to remedy this offers a stable foundation for financial products, improving safety and trust. Lenders looking for reliable collateral can now use familiar assets, creating a new trust between traditional finance and the crypto world.

Recent collaboration in this space is turning heads. Initiatives like Ondo Finance are paving the way for new financial products backed by US treasuries. By teaming up with established asset managers such as BlackRock, Ondo is proving that the old guard can indeed play well with the new kids on the block. Their offerings promise not just accessibility but also credibility. This is not just a flash in the pan; it's a solid strategy that could usher in a new wave of investment paradigms given the changing macroeconomic atmosphere. With a rise in inflation in recent years Ondo looks to capitalize on higher interest rates as an attractive option to grow capital going forward in this space.

Similarly, platforms like Centrifuge are creating pathways that allow users to leverage their physical assets as collateral for loans. Imagine needing cash flow for your business and instantly using your outstanding invoices or real estate as collateral without the red tape. This transformation streamlines borrowing, making what was once cumbersome, a breeze. Centrifuge's dual-token system further enhances this interaction, ensuring that governance and financial stability are not mutually exclusive.

Let's not forget the original in the real world asset sector, stablecoins. Like USDC and Tether, stablecoins serve as links between fiat currency and crypto, offering a range of utility in the decentralized finance world. These assets can be seen as real world assets as they are pegged to the US Dollar, and they can be utilized in various applications including staking for interest. Also, during periods of market turbulence these assets allow users to maintain purchasing power without cashing out. With the increased adoption of stablecoins in decentralized finance platforms, we're seeing their role evolve from mere digital dollars to indispensable tools that empower broader financial inclusivity.

The ongoing development of real world assets signals a shift towards a more resilient financial system. By connecting the dots between traditional assets and blockchain technologies, these innovations are breathing new life into investment strategies, broadening wealth building opportunities for various demographics. Just as the internet sparked a revolution across multiple industries, real world assets stand to disrupt and redefine conventional finance, commodities, and real estate.

As we look toward the future, the promise of accessibility, transparency, and enhanced liquidity offers a glimpse into a more inclusive financial world. Just as we saw with the democratization of information with the innovation of the internet this new frontier in finance propels us toward a future where financial barriers dissolve, and opportunities abound. So as the landscape is changing, tangible assets offer a solid foundation for a sustainable evolution in wealth creation for everyone.

Chapter 4: The Crypto Gaming Revolution

Imagine a virtual world where players own their digital assets across all games, trading them as they would or simply accumulating their favorite skins. That's the dream of the crypto gaming revolution! With blockchain technology paving the way players can now claim ownership of their in game items allowing a once passive experience to be more interactive and valuable.

The emergence of play-to-earn models and non-fungible tokens has disrupted traditional gaming economics. Players can earn valuable digital assets that are no longer confined to a single game but can be bought, sold, and traded across different platforms. The ability to transition digital assets among games has unleashed a wave of liquidity previously unheard of in gaming.

The term 'play-to-earn' really captures the essence of this new direction, appealing not just to die-hard gamers but to a wide spectrum of players looking to monetize their skills across the world. The average player in countries with low value fiat currencies can play video games as a legitimate means of earning income. However, as enticing as this seems, it's essential to acknowledge the challenges lurking beneath the surface.

Just like a poker game, the thrill can quickly turn to disaster if you're not careful. The initial excitement surrounding blockchain games led to a flurry of projects, but some that were once riding high on investor enthusiasm now find themselves grappling with performance issues and dwindling player engagement, like Decentraland.

Now, industry insiders are keen to prioritize compelling gameplay over quick profits. The new focus is on creating games that offer stunning graphics and gameplay mechanics comparable to AAA titles like Call of Duty. After all, encouraging players to invest time and money in lackluster experiences isn't a sustainable strategy. A promising example of breaking through the noise is "Off The Grid." It is a blockchain game that has captured more and more users with its engaging survival and strategy elements set in a dystopian future. In this game, players can create unique characters, manage resources, and explore an intricately designed open world. What's more, "Off The Grid" allows players to own in game assets via non-fungible tokens, enabling them to buy, sell, and trade those assets in a peer-to-peer marketplace.

Projects like Superverse are leading the charge in the gaming space by combining non-fungible tokens with immersive gameplay. Superverse offers players an experience where in game items are tokenized and their play-to-earn system is designed to reward players for their time and effort, fostering an ecosystem that thrives on continual engagement. However, it's important to realize the value of the Superverse token is mainly governance and offers little else in the way of gaming since Superverse is still waiting on an AAA game to bolster its ecosystem. You should know that governance tokens do not provide any extra utility besides, well, governing or voting on matters about Superverse.

Let's also discuss Immutable X, which addresses crucial issues surrounding scalability and transaction efficiency. Operating as a layer-2 solution on Ethereum that is focused on gaming it enables instant transactions without gas fees resolving one of the significant barriers in blockchain gaming. The partnership with well-known games like "Gods Unchained" further cements its commitment to enhancing player ownership while driving community interaction through exclusive rewards and tradable items.

However, as with any investment, there are risks involved. The cryptocurrency gaming sector is like navigating through a jungle to find treasure, with enormous potential there are plenty of pitfalls and predators. Many gaming projects while they may possess the potential to be a good investment may fall short of achieving their goals as with any company. Players and investors alike must practice due diligence, keeping their ear to the ground for news and updates from credible sources. Staying connected to community driven sources on platforms like Discord or Twitter can also provide insights that aid in making informed decisions.

As we look to the future, the fusion of blockchain technology with the creative world of gaming offers a new playground for both developers and players, ushering in an era where entertainment meets economic empowerment. Whether you're looking to profit or just enjoy the game, the crypto gaming world is transforming lives and redefining how we think about the digital economy.

Chapter 5: Decentralized Finance

As we step into the world of decentralized finance, we're opening a door to a financial landscape that's reshaping how we think about money and transactions. Imagine a world where anyone can lend, borrow, or trade without the need for banks or fees. That's the charm of decentralized finance, it's like setting up a global market where everybody gets to interact through smart contracts directly and trustlessly on blockchain technology.

As stated before, decentralized finance works by removing intermediaries, offering a seamless alternative to traditional finance paperwork and wait times. Instead of relying on institutions to handle our transactions, decentralized finance relies on self executing smart contracts with the terms of the agreement directly written into code. Smart contracts are like automated restaurants that execute the cooking process flawlessly, once they put in the ingredients and press start the contract is fulfilled and the dish prepared exactly as specified, without any risk of misinterpreting the order.

Key applications driving the decentralized finance revolution include lending and borrowing protocols, decentralized exchanges, and yield farming. Lending and borrowing are pivotal functions within decentralized finance. Platforms like Aave and Compound allow users to lend their cryptocurrencies and earn interest on their holdings. Lending and borrowing protocols are like having a personal garden where your money can grow. You plant your funds in fertile soil, nurture them with interest, and harvest the fruits of your labor whenever you need them without dealing with any middlemen or bureaucratic red tape. Such platforms essentially create a peer-to-peer lending environment, eliminating excessive fees and promoting financial transparency. One pitfall of lending and borrowing protocols is the fluctuation in interest rates determined by market conditions that can mean inconsistent returns for the lender. Borrowers in lending protocols face the risk of being liquidated if the value of their collateral falls below a certain loan to value threshold, potentially leading to the loss of their staked assets if they are unable to repay the loan on time. A borrower can also add collateral to decrease the loan to value ratio to appease the threshold. Perhaps lending and borrowing protocols will leverage real world assets as collateral in the future to reduce these risks.

Moonwell is emerging as a decentralized lending protocol that prioritizes community governance and engagement. Moonwell is not only fostering a user-centric approach but is also ensuring that decisions regarding the protocol evolve through community input. Its commitment to rigorous security audits signals a focus on building trust among users, making it an exciting project to watch as decentralized finance continues to expand. One of the reasons for mentioning Moonwell is the tested utility it brings to the crypto space as with other lending protocols, moreover, it has a market cap a fraction of the size of Aave and Compound meaning there is plenty of room for growth.

Now let's look at decentralized exchanges, unlike traditional platforms decentralized exchanges like Uniswap and SushiSwap allow users to trade directly from their wallets instantly without intermediaries. It's like trading with friends, your rules in your smart contracts, exchanging tokens without the burden of central authorities. While this model enhances accessibility and reduces trading costs, it does come with several pitfalls. One major risk associated with liquidity pools on decentralized exchanges is impermanent loss. This occurs when you lose value in assets simply because the price of the asset drops while it is staked in the liquidity pool. As a result, investors could experience decreased returns or even outright losses, highlighting the risks involved in providing liquidity to a decentralized exchange.

Yield farming has taken the crypto world by storm, allowing users to earn rewards by providing liquidity to various protocols. Yield farming is akin to deploying capital into a nutrient-rich ecosystem to provide liquidity in return for higher than normal yields. By depositing assets into a decentralized finance platform, you earn yields that might outpace traditional savings accounts by leaps and bounds. However, as anyone who's participated in yield farming knows, you have to be careful with what you whip up in the kitchen. Often yield farming is necessary for tokens due to their lack of liquidity in certain pairings, and while the yields can be tempting they often come with risks like smart contract vulnerabilities or highly speculative tokens that could turn sour overnight.

A critical piece of the decentralized finance puzzle is the tokenization of physical assets like real estate, art, or even invoices to be seamlessly traded on blockchain platforms. Imagine being able to own a fraction of a high-rise building in Manhattan, all while lounging at home in the country. Platforms like RealT and Centrifuge are leading the charge, actively promoting fractional ownership and improving liquidity in assets that were once deemed illiquid and exclusive to the rich.

It's not all rainbows and sunshine, though. The decentralized finance landscape is full of challenges. Market volatility, regulatory scrutiny, and security risks continue to pose significant threats. For instance, many programs have experienced hacks that left investors in shock at the loss of their funds. This reality underscores the need for due diligence and staying informed about the evolving landscape. The decentralized finance space is still young, with innovative projects emerging almost daily. As various platforms continue to adapt and evolve the anticipation of better user experiences and broader adoption is inevitable. These developments signify an essential shift toward a more inclusive financial infrastructure where accessibility and transparency reign supreme.

As we move forward, embracing decentralized finance's potential hinges on understanding its intricacies. The opportunities are vast, but they require a willingness to learn and adapt in a fast-paced environment. Whether you're a seasoned investor or a curious newcomer, the world of decentralized finance invites you to explore the road where traditional finance meets innovation in new ways.

Chapter 6: Meme Coins
High Risk, High Reward

Ah, meme coins, those quirky little tokens that took the crypto world by storm, often born from jokes but now serious players in the market. If you've ever scrolled through social media and stumbled upon the iconic Doge meme, you're already familiar with one of the biggest names in this arena, Dogecoin. Picture a digital currency that started as a lighthearted nod to an internet meme, now boasting a market cap approaching a staggering $13.85 billion. It's like finding out the goofy picture of a Shiba Inu you chuckled at could make you rich!

Meme coins often thrive on humor, irony, and social media trends, enticing investors with promises of astronomical returns. In many ways, investing in these coins can be as exhilarating as a wild roller coaster with unexpected twists and turns. The allure of quick profits on social media, can transform a simple tweet into a financial phenomenon overnight. Never underestimate the power of the crowd and communities rallying around meme coins, creating a whirlwind of engagement that fuels their popularity is a prime example of the network effect.

However, with great reward comes great risk. The volatility associated with meme coins is nothing short of legendary. Their value can skyrocket in a matter of hours, only to plummet just as quickly. This kind of unpredictability can make even seasoned investors sweat bullets. You might start your day smiling at a significant profit, only to find yourself in the red by lunchtime. When investing in these coins, it's essential to maintain a level head. Meme coins should be traded differently than most cryptos, where a simple HODL strategy is most likely not in your best interest, instead, swing trading to capture the momentum when a meme coin is pumping suits the volatility of meme coins. Websites like Dexscreener.com can be helpful tools in picking out those pumping meme coins and while there are meme coins on many blockchains the undisputed king of meme coin markets lies on the Solana blockchain.

Another of the more stable meme coins leading the charge alongside Dogecoin is Shiba Inu, which is crafted on the Ethereum blockchain and backed by an enthusiastic community known as the "Shiba Army." They engage in decentralized finance, enhancing SHIB's appeal with liquidity pools and staking options that allow users to earn passive income. Investing in SHIB can feel like being part of a bustling community thriving on collaboration and shared interests. But just like any meme coin, it has its share of risks and challenges that need to be navigated with caution.

And let's not overlook FLOKI, named after Elon Musk's dog. This ambitious project aims not just for meme status but seeks to forge its way into the non-fungible token gaming sphere while developing decentralized finance products. With aspirations running high, FLOKI is an excellent example of how meme coins can try to morph into more serious projects while still maintaining their fun roots. Entering the meme coin space isn't as straightforward as plopping down your money. Many tokens thrive outside the mainstream exchanges and require a bit more finesse to acquire. Here's a simplified playbook on how to successfully snag these elusive assets:

1. Use Decentralized Exchanges: Many meme coins are available on decentralized platforms like Uniswap, SushiSwap, or PancakeSwap. You'll need a compatible wallet (think MetaMask or Trust Wallet) and the appropriate currency, Ethereum for Uniswap or Binance Smart Chain for PancakeSwap.

2. Connect Your Wallet: Navigate to your chosen exchange's website to connect your wallet, making sure to grant permission when prompted by your wallet.

3. Choose the Pairing on the Exchange: Determine which tokens to trade (for example, DOGE/ETH for buying Dogecoin using Ethereum or SHIB/USDC for buying Shiba Inu using USDC).

4. Confirm the Transaction: Specify how much you want to buy, but keep an eye on transaction fees that can surge when networks are congested. Sometimes, those costs go from a couple of bucks to several hundred, so make sure to do your homework!

5. Stay Updated: It's crucial to conduct thorough research on the projects before investing. Engage in community discussions, monitor social

media channels, and check out the official Twitch, Discord, or Reddit pages to stay in the loop.

Investing in meme coins is undeniably a thrilling venture, yet for every success story, there are cautionary tales. Scams, pump-and-dump schemes, and poorly managed projects can easily lead inexperienced investors down a rocky path. To get an idea of their legitimacy before investing check third-party audits, like Go+ Security, Quik Intel, or Token Sniffer for meme coins, and also check the meme coins website. The key is not to dive in headfirst; instead, tread carefully and gather as much information as possible before making any moves.

Just like navigating a minefield, becoming educated about the crypto landscape can help you avoid pitfalls. Whether you're drawn to meme culture, motivated by the thrill of potential profits, or want to be part of a growing community meme coins make it possible.

Chapter 7: AI Cryptocurrencies

Artificial intelligence is intersecting with blockchain technology to reshape industries and redefine how we think about digital assets. As artificial intelligence continues to advance, its integration with blockchains opens up exciting opportunities, offering innovative solutions to real world problems and fostering a new wave of applications that extend well beyond the financial world. Below will highlight a few projects that are gaining traction in this sector.

Bittensor is one standout project in this space pioneering a decentralized neural network. Imagine a community of developers and computing enthusiasts sharing their resources and enhancing artificial intelligence models that can be used in various applications like language processing and predictive analytics. Bittensor's uniqueness lies in its ability to allow participants to contribute computing power and data for training 'machine learning models'. Through this network, individuals can earn rewards in the form of TAO, the project's native token. Bittensor democratizes access to powerful artificial intelligence tools, allowing anyone with computing resources to engage in this growing ecosystem.

Similarly, Render is making waves by transforming how rendering services are accessed and utilized. Render empowers artists and developers by giving them the tools they need to harness the power of artificial intelligence to optimize rendering workflows and output quality. This decentralized network connects digital artists and developers seeking unused GPU computational power for rendering solutions. In an era where demands for stunning visuals in gaming, film, and virtual reality are at an all time high, the native RNDR token is simplifying access to rendering capabilities while reducing costs.

Another noteworthy project dedicated to enhancing supply chain transparency and data integrity through its innovative approach is OriginTrail. By employing artificial intelligence algorithms, OriginTrail analyzes and validates data from various sources ensuring that retailers, consumers, and manufacturers have access to reliable information about product origins and handling processes. The network's ability to create a decentralized knowledge graph means that products can be traced from raw materials to the end consumer. This capability addresses some of the critical challenges in today's complex global supply chains, where the intricacies of sourcing and production are often untraceable. With the native TRAC token facilitating these data exchanges, OriginTrail represents a movement toward more responsible and sustainable business practices in an increasingly connected world.

Numerai, a hedge fund that gathers financial machine learning models from data scientists around the world, created Numeraire. Numeraire tokens can be staked by these data scientists who submit their predictions to influence how the fund invests. By leveraging artificial intelligence, these data scientists analyze vast datasets and market trends to develop sophisticated models that improve the accuracy of their predictions. This system aligns their interests with the fund's success because they are rewarded based on how well their predictions perform. This innovative approach demonstrates how artificial intelligence can have a real impact on financial markets.

Then there's Fetch.ai, a platform designed to empower autonomous agents capable of carrying out tasks on behalf of users. By combining artificial intelligence, machine learning, and blockchain technology, Fetch.ai supports the development of decentralized applications that improve resource management, enable efficient data sharing, and automate a wide array of tasks. This functionality is especially valuable in sectors such as transportation and logistics, where optimizing routes and managing supply chains can lead to significant cost savings and enhanced efficiency. Artificial intelligence agents are a very interesting breakthrough in digital capabilities, with the possibility to disrupt the world with efficiency.

With artificial intelligence cryptocurrencies it becomes clear that these projects represent a vision for a future where collaboration, transparency, and efficiency take center stage. These initiatives continue to unlock unprecedented possibilities empowering individuals and organizations alike to harness their potential in creating sustainable solutions that enhance the way we live, work, and transact. The future is bright for artificial intelligence cryptocurrencies, and their journey has only just begun. With their potential to revolutionize how we interact with data, build trust, and manage resources, artificial intelligence cryptocurrencies are poised for significant growth in the coming years.

Chapter 8: Pitfalls of Crypto Bull Markets

The thrill of a cryptocurrency bull market can feel as exhilarating as riding a wild stallion across open fields, freedom, excitement, and potential profits leap like frogs into a pond. Beneath all that lies a tangled web of risks that can ensnare both novice and seasoned traders. It's essential to understand that while the allure of soaring prices whispers sweet nothings to your wallet, it can also lead to devastating losses if you are not careful.

One of the biggest pitfalls during a bull run is the infamous "fear of missing out." You've likely encountered it as prices surge and the headlines tout new all-time highs, many investors leap headfirst into the market, driven more by excitement than by strategy. Remember for every buyer driving up the price there are sellers taking profits, resulting in buyers holding the bag. It's a bit like a group of friends diving into a pool, the splash is great, but you might just hit the shallow end. Many who succumb to the "fear of missing out" buy assets at inflated prices before grappling with significant losses as the tide inevitably turns and the price corrects. Employing dollar cost averaging, where you invest a fixed amount regularly regardless of market conditions, helps mitigate the risk of buying assets at overblown prices. This more thoughtful approach can be a lifesaver for an investor, doing research and investing only what you can afford to lose can also help you navigate these turbulent waters.

Investors who take the time to explore the background of a coin or token are likely to find themselves better equipped to make sound decisions amid the bull run. Analyzing its utility, team, and market trends instead of rushing in during price surges can save you from making poor investment decisions. For instance, to analyze the utility of a token, research a coin to determine if the cryptocurrency can bring value to people's lives and consider whether this is something many people need or would use. Checking LinkedIn can be a great way to verify a project's team for red flags or strong credentials. Finally, understanding market's need volume to make significant moves can help illustrate how understanding market conditions is pivotal when analyzing the soundness of an investment. Think of it as climbing a mountain, taking analytical steps is often a far better strategy than sprinting ahead and risking a nasty fall.

Bull markets can also attract the worst kind of individuals, scammers. The wave of excitement often invites shady characters looking to exploit unwary investors. Just like a thief in the night, these con artists can launch Ponzi schemes, phishing attacks, and deceptive projects to gain users' funds. The best defense against these scams? Conduct thorough due diligence, investigate the project's team, technology, and community feedback to ensure you're not stepping into a trap.

Another common pitfall occurs when investors avoid securing their wallets or accounts. Revealing your seed phrase can be like handing a thief the key to your home, it could lead to instant and irreversible losses. Your seed phrase is your key to your wallet, for your eyes only, and should be memorized or kept in a secure place. Moreover, failing to adopt proper security measures, like enabling two-factor authentication can leave you vulnerable to unauthorized access. Making emotional trading decisions, buying enthusiastically in the face of rising prices or panic-selling during downturns, can also wreak havoc on your portfolio. A level headed strategy, coupled with a sense of a tokens community through platforms like Twitter, Reddit, or Discord can bolster knowledge and reinforce best practices.

Market volatility is another shadow lurking during bull runs. While most crypto critics call the inherent volatility a 'bug' many crypto investors revel in the opportunities provided by increased market volatility. Keep in mind price rallies can lead to incredible profits, but the increased volatility means equally rapid declines. Think of it as a high-stakes poker game where players can leave rich one moment and bankrupt the next hand. Taking profits along the way is easier said than done, but will ensure that you do not leave empty handed. Once again a simple level headed strategy like dollar cost averaging out can help an investor unsure of when to pull out their profits. History shows that Bitcoin often undergoes steep corrections during bull markets. In previous bull markets declines of 20% to 30% after major rises are common, with some traders finding that sudden market corrections can erase significant gains overnight only to be up again in the next few days. These corrections can offer a great opportunity to add to positions for the next leg up in the bull run, however, once crypto has a significant rally be cautious about investing near all time highs with decreasing volume. Other indicators can be used to help identify the bull run cycle top, remember, bull markets don't last forever. Taking a look at Glassnode.com charts when analyzing Bitcoin cycle tops can reveal several key indicators and metrics often utilized to maximize profits at cycle tops:

1. Realized Price: This chart shows the average price at which all Bitcoin in circulation was last moved. When the market price significantly exceeds the realized price, it can indicate overvaluation and a potential peak in the cycle.

2. MVRV Ratio: The Market Value to Realized Value ratio compares Bitcoin's market capitalization to its realized capitalization. An MVRV significantly above 3 typically suggests that Bitcoin is overbought and may indicate a cycle top.

3. Puell Multiple: This metric assesses the daily issuance of Bitcoin in USD terms relative to its historical average. High Puell Multiple values above 4 indicate that miners are generating revenue that is much higher than normal, which may coincide with market peaks.

4. NVT Ratio: The Network Value to Transactions Ratio compares Bitcoin's market capitalization to its transaction volume. A rising NVT ratio suggests a disconnect between the increasing market price and the actual utility of the network, often signaling a peak.

5. Inactive Supply: Charts that track the percentage of Bitcoin supply that has been inactive for a long period can provide insights into potential market behavior; a spike in dormant supply being moved at high prices may suggest speculative interest and potential cycle tops.

6.Accumulation vs. Distribution: These charts illustrate whether BTC is being accumulated or distributed by long-term holders versus short-term traders. An increase in distribution at high prices may signal a cycle top as long-term holders sell into market strength.

7.Exchange Inflows and Outflows: Monitoring the net flow of BTC into and out of exchanges can give insight into market sentiment. Significant inflows at elevated prices often indicate selling pressure, suggesting a potential peak.

Having achievable expectations and a robust risk management plan, including stop-loss orders, will help protect portfolios during times of uncertainty. Agreements to maintain realistic views about potential gains help mitigate the risk of emotional decisions based on market hype. Previous bull runs have seen most cryptocurrencies conservatively double or triple in value, while the biggest movers can provide hundreds or thousands of multiples in returns. Awareness of market psychology and a firm grasp of your risks are paramount to reaping the rewards without losing your head.

Despite these challenges, bull markets offer exciting opportunities for skilled swing traders and long-term investors alike. By understanding market rhythms, careful strategizing, and adopting a proactive approach to risk management, you can position yourself to thrive in these environments. A mix of caution and enthusiasm will be necessary for your navigation of cryptocurrency Investments.

Chapter 9: Tokenomics and Key Crypto Indicators

In the game of cryptocurrency investment, one key aspect of critical importance is thorough research and analysis before diving into any project. It's much like preparing for a treasure hunt, understanding the map, and the risks can mean the difference between striking gold or walking away empty handed. Investors should keep a keen eye on key elements such as tokenomics, the qualifications of the development team, token unlock schedules, and the availability of clear project documentation.

Tokenomics serve as the backbone of any cryptocurrency, providing insight into the economic model that determines how the tokens function. Take Bitcoin for example, with a capped supply of 21 million coins its scarcity is designed through periodic halving events, which reduce the rate of new coins entering circulation per block by half. This creates an anti-inflationary asset environment earning Bitcoin its nickname, "digital gold." Another important part of Bitcoin tokenomics is the circulating supply, which directly affects the price as roughly 19 million of the 21 million Bitcoins are currently circulating with the other 2 million yet to be mined Bitcoins dilution is reaching maturation. It is important to know that a cryptocurrency with a low circulating supply is susceptible to dilution in price as the circulating supply increases, similar to a company issuing more stock.

On the other hand, Sui, another up and coming layer one blockchain showcases a different approach to tokenomics. With incentives geared towards community participation, Sui aims to create a sustainable growth model without the same rigid limits as Bitcoin. The dynamics of its supply is approximately 3 billion tokens are circulating now with a maximum cap of 10 billion tokens. With consistent unlocks scheduled over the next few years users should be aware of the downward price pressure that comes with the increase in circulating supply. Projects implement token unlocks to incentivize early investors and align their interests with the long term success of the project. Sometimes the unlocking schedules are gradual, like Sui, and minimally affect price action, but other projects like Ondo Finance have a token unlock coming up that will double the circulating supply, theoretically cutting the price in half. Unlock schedules are a crucial component to monitor when considering the time and percentage of tokens unlocked, along with the price paid for those tokens by early investors and team members. Paying attention to this is important since no one wants to be left holding the bag from a spiral of selling pressure after a large unlock.

As mentioned earlier, an essential aspect of exploring any cryptocurrency is examining the team behind the project. A well-structured team comprised of industry veterans is often a hallmark of a promising project. By investigating their backgrounds, experience in successful startups, or contributions to established financial institutions investors can gauge the project's credibility. A cryptocurrency with a team that boasts successful previous endeavors is likely to tackle challenges more effectively, than a team with little experience in the blockchain or technology space.

The project's website also plays an important role as its public face. Think of it as a first date, if the website looks appealing and is easy to navigate you're more likely to be impressed. For instance, Sui's website offers an organized presentation of its tokenomics, roadmap, and functionalities, ensuring transparency and accessibility for investors. Red flags to look for on a project's website are lack of clarity, information that is not up to date or lacking, as well as a lack or deterioration of social media presence across the various platforms. Checking social media platforms for up to date posting and activity is a good way to keep one's finger on a project's pulse, which brings us to a side note about knowing when to cut your losses. Cryptocurrency projects are born and die every day, be aware that when a crypto trades at very low volume or has significantly decreasing activity there is a point where if a project is dying it can be best practice to cut your losses and move on.

Reading the whitepaper, which outlines the cryptocurrency's vision and operational mechanics, is like reading the rulebook for a game. Bitcoin's whitepaper vision was the need for a decentralized peer-to-peer cash system while its operational mechanics are the proof-of-work mechanism. Comparatively, Sui's whitepaper goes into detail about its unique proof-of-stake mechanism designed to handle transactions in parallel. The clarity and depth of these documents matter immensely, as well articulated ideas and thought out plans signal a project's commitment to becoming a viable player in the crypto space.

A vibrant community can also signal a cryptocurrency's potential for growth. A strong user base not only bolsters the project's viability but also helps create a feedback loop that can improve and adapt the cryptocurrency over time. Bitcoin boasts a loyal and active community that promotes knowledge sharing and can help newcomers navigate the complex waters of crypto investing. In contrast, newer projects like Sui have much to gain from active engagement and feedback as they continue to determine their niches in this competitive environment.

Market positioning and performance metrics like market capitalization and to reiterate, trading volume plays a pivotal role in assessing future viability. A larger market cap often signifies an established status in the market, which can provide confidence to potential investors but may limit the upside price potential. Once again, trading volume is an important thing to watch as it signals the popularity of a cryptocurrency at any given time. Keep in mind during prime market conditions volume is crucial for a large price rally. Analyzing price history and trends, alongside understanding broader narratives in crypto allows for more precise readings of what lies ahead for any given cryptocurrency.

The path to invest in a cryptocurrency should be lined with valuable data and insights. By diligently evaluating tokenomics, the development team, unlock schedules, and community engagement, astute investors can enhance their chances of identifying sustainable projects ripe for growth.

With reliable resources at hand, anyone can embark on a thoughtful journey through the intricacies of the cryptocurrency market, leading to more informed decisions and potentially rewarding outcomes.

RESOURCE LIST:

Understanding Tokenomics
Resources: CoinMarketcap.com Messari.com

Investigating Token Unlocks
Resources: TokenUnlocks.com

Assessing the Team and Development
Resources: LinkedIn, official project website

Evaluating the Website and User Experience
Resources: Official project websites, Trustpilot

Reviewing the Whitepaper
Resources: Official project website, GitHub, whitepaper repositories

Exploring Community and Ecosystem Engagement
Resources: Reddit, Telegram groups, Discord servers, Twitter

Analyzing Market Position and Comparison
Resources: CoinGecko, Dune Analytics, Glassnode.com

This summary provides an overview of the key resources that can be utilized for in-depth analysis across various aspects of cryptocurrency evaluation.

Chapter 10: Looking Ahead

The winds of change are blowing through the cryptocurrency markets, and the future looks promising. By the end of 2025, we can expect significant transformations influenced by a blend of macroeconomic factors, technological innovations, regulatory frameworks, and evolving global monetary policies. It's like gearing up for a thrilling race with various obstacles and opportunities awaiting every turn.

Predictions for the global cryptocurrency market forecast a compound annual growth rate of around 31% based on past performance. Picture more individuals, businesses, and institutions integrating cryptocurrencies into their financial playbooks. Bitcoin, still reigning as the king of cryptocurrencies, is expected to lead the charge. Analysts say Bitcoin could potentially reach values between $100,000 and $200,000 by the end of 2025. This prediction isn't just wishful thinking, it's fueled by increasing adoption, tech advancements, and rising inflation pressures on traditional currencies. Bitcoin is increasingly seen as a digital safeguard with many looking for a safe haven against inflation similar to gold, although Bitcoin does trade like a risk asset often coinciding with the stock market. For years Bitcoin users have expected a decoupling from traditional asset markets, but the cryptocurrency market has been similarly tied to the rise and fall of global liquidity like traditional markets.

One of the key macroeconomic influences here is the bold monetary policy being adopted by central banks worldwide. As these institutions lower interest rates and expand the money supply in response to economic turmoil, concerns about inflation begin to creep in. With people more anxious about the devaluation of fiat currencies, the interest in digital assets is gaining traction. Just imagine a time when more and more people turn to cryptocurrencies not just for investment, but as a reliable store of value. Bitcoin has outperformed every other asset class over the last 10 years, hands down no questions asked, and it looks to continue this trend.

At the same time, the rise of Central Bank Digital Currencies is redefining the landscape of finance. Countries are exploring their digital currency options to modernize payment systems and improve financial inclusion. Some argue that central bank digital currencies will lend legitimacy to the digital currency sphere, ultimately fostering a more comprehensive financial ecosystem. It's like watching a new player enter the crypto game and realizing their skills can complement rather than compete with the existing environment.

Technological innovations are set to play a pivotal role in shaping cryptocurrency markets as well. Enhancements in artificial intelligence are already making waves, paving the way for more efficient trading strategies, improved security protocols via predictive algorithms, and overall enhanced user experiences. Imagine using AI to fine-tune your trading approach, capitalizing on market trends before they even become apparent. One of the most recent artificial intelligence developments is AI agents. An AI agent is a software program that utilizes artificial intelligence techniques to autonomously perform tasks, make decisions, and interact with users or other systems in real time. Potential use cases for AI agents include customer support chatbots that provide instant assistance, virtual personal assistants that manage schedules and tasks, and intelligent systems that analyze data in various industries, such as finance and healthcare.

Another technological innovation, quantum computing, presents both potential benefits and challenges. Its remarkable processing power may help improve security and transaction processing speeds, but it also poses risks to existing cryptographic algorithms. Quantum computers are particularly valuable for specific use cases, such as cryptography, complex simulations, and optimization problems where their unique ability to process vast amounts of data simultaneously can significantly outperform classical computers. Cryptos like Bitcoin, which rely on SHA-256 encryption, could find themselves in hot water if quantum solutions are not adopted. Also an interesting fact about the capabilities of quantum computers to break the cryptography of hardware wallets; it would take 173 sextillion years for a quantum computer to guess a 12 word seed phrase from a 2000 word seed phrase bank assuming it is guessing a billion outcomes per second, which they are not capable of yet. So, while it might be years before quantum computing has the capabilities to break cryptography, it's something developers need to be proactive about.

Decentralized finance is continually evolving to meet the needs of its users, often crossing banking boundaries. As decentralized finance platforms advance, we'll see increased interactivity between traditional and decentralized systems, enabling broader access to innovative financial tools. Innovations such as yield farming, decentralized insurance, and non-fungible token marketplaces will likely become mainstays in the financial toolkit for everyone from casual investors to large institutions.

Alongside these trends are challenges in the regulatory arena, where governments are beginning to recognize the necessity for clear guidelines to protect consumers while promoting growth within the cryptocurrency space. Currently, cryptocurrency faces significant regulatory challenges globally, particularly regarding the need for clearer frameworks to define and classify digital assets, which can differ dramatically from one jurisdiction to another. Key regulatory bodies, such as the U.S. Securities and Exchange Commission and the European Union's Markets in Crypto-Assets initiative, are actively working to establish comprehensive guidelines that not only facilitate innovation but also address critical issues like anti-money laundering compliance, taxation, and investor protection. As governments and regulatory authorities worldwide seek to adapt their frameworks to the rapidly evolving digital asset landscape, the outcome of their efforts will significantly shape the future of cryptocurrency markets and influence how stakeholders navigate this growing space.

The total cryptocurrency market cap is approximately $1.2 trillion, showing signs of recovery and renewed interest in digital assets following previous downturns. Analysts predict that over the decade, the market cap could soar to between $5 trillion and $10 trillion, driven by increasing institutional adoption, advancements in blockchain technology, and the expansion of decentralized finance applications. For instance, a recent survey by Fidelity found that 70% of institutional investors believe that digital assets will play a significant role in the future of finance, highlighting a growing confidence in the sector. Additionally, the rise of central bank digital currencies and regulatory clarity in major markets are expected to further enhance the legitimacy and integration of cryptocurrencies within the global financial ecosystem. With these factors in play, the trajectory of the cryptocurrency market appears promising, potentially leading to substantial growth in its overall capitalization.

Navigating this exciting yet unpredictable world means staying adaptable. With new projects emerging, technologies evolving, and regulations changing, those who remain informed and agile will thrive. It's a thrilling time to be engaged in the cryptocurrency sphere, as the dynamics of traditional finance and decentralized systems merge for a potentially transformative journey.

List of Cryptocurrencies Mentioned

1. Bitcoin (BTC)

- Decentralization: Bitcoin operates on a peer-to-peer network, allowing transactions without intermediaries like banks or government authorities.
- Scarcity: With a capped supply of 21 million coins, Bitcoin's scarcity is designed to drive value, making it often referred to as "digital gold."
- Proof-of-Work: Bitcoin uses a proof-of-work consensus mechanism, where miners validate transactions by solving complex mathematical problems, which contributes to its security.

2. Ethereum (ETH)

- Smart Contracts: Ethereum allows the creation of decentralized applications and smart contracts, enabling automated transactions without intermediaries.
- Transition to Proof-of-Stake: Ethereum is moving from a proof-of-work model to a proof-of-stake system (Ethereum 2.0), which aims to be more energy-efficient and scalable.
- Large Ecosystem: It has a vast ecosystem, supporting hundreds of tokens and dApps, making it a leading platform in the decentralized finance space.

3. Solana (SOL)

- High Throughput: Solana boasts fast transaction speeds and low fees, capable of processing thousands of transactions per second through its unique proof-of-history mechanism.
- Decentralized Applications: The platform supports various decentralized finance applications, gaming, and NFT projects, facilitating a diverse ecosystem.

- Mainstream Partnerships: Collaborations with major companies like Google Cloud indicate growing recognition and adoption in traditional markets.

4. Shiba Inu (SHIB)

- Meme Coin: Initially created as a joke in response to Dogecoin's popularity, it has developed a substantial community known as the "Shiba Army."
- Decentralized Finance Features: Shiba Inu incorporates decentralized finance elements, allowing users to participate in liquidity pools and staking activities.
- Market Presence: Despite concerns about its volatility, it remains popular due to its vibrant community and marketing strategies.

5. Dogecoin (DOGE)

- Originating as a Joke: Dogecoin started as a meme but gained traction, becoming a widely recognized cryptocurrency and a favorite among fans of cryptocurrency culture.
- Community-Driven: It has a strong and dedicated community that supports various charitable causes and promotes its use.
- Low Transaction Fees: Dogecoin allows users to make transactions at low costs, which contributes to its appeal for microtransactions and tipping.

6. Floki (FLOKI)

- Named After Elon Musk's Dog: FLOKI is inspired by the Shiba Inu dog of Elon Musk, combining meme culture with ambitions to establish a more serious position in the crypto market.
- NFT and Gaming Focus: Beyond being a meme coin, FLOKI is looking to expand into the gaming industry and NFTs, promoting liquidity and community-oriented projects.
- Community Engagement: The FLOKI project boasts a passionate community focused on expanding its ecosystem and introducing new use cases.

7. Sui (SUI)

- Tokenomics and Scaling: Sui features unique tokenomics with a maximum cap of 10 billion tokens and explores effective scaling solutions to accommodate growth.
- Upcoming Unlocks: The scheduled unlocks for token distribution are critical to its market dynamics, affecting liquidity and price.
- Platform Foundations: Sui aims to provide a solid foundation for decentralized applications, focusing on community participation and robust transactional capabilities.

8. Centrifuge (CFG)

- Bridging Real-World Assets: Centrifuge allows users to leverage their physical assets as collateral for loans, facilitating increased liquidity for previously illiquid assets.
- Dual-Token System: The platform utilizes a dual-token system that serves governance and utility purposes, creating a balanced approach to user engagement.
- Community Focus: By enabling the tokenization of real-world assets, Centrifuge promotes a community-driven model that empowers users.

9. Uniswap (UNI)

- Decentralized Exchange: Uniswap is a widely used decentralized exchange that facilitates automated trading of Ethereum-based tokens.
- Automated Market Making: Utilizing an automated market-making system, users can trade directly from their wallets without the need for an order book.
- Liquidity Pools: Uniswap allows individuals to provide liquidity and earn rewards, which incentivizes broader participation in the ecosystem.

10. SushiSwap (SUSHI)

- Community-Driven DEX: SushiSwap is a decentralized exchange modeled after Uniswap, with a focus on community engagement and governance through its native token, SUSHI.
- Yield Farming Opportunities: The platform offers yield farming and staking options, making it attractive for users looking to optimize returns on their liquidity.
- Cross-Chain Compatibility: SushiSwap aims for cross-chain capabilities, broadening its reach and accessibility within the decentralized finance space.

11. Aave (AAVE)

- Lending and Borrowing Protocol: Aave is a decentralized lending protocol that allows users to lend and borrow a variety of cryptocurrencies in a secure environment.
- Flash Loans: Aave popularized flash loans, enabling users to borrow funds without collateral as long as the borrowed amount is returned within one transaction.
- Interest Rate Models: The platform features innovative interest rate models that adapt based on market conditions, providing transparency for users.

12. Compound (COMP)

- Algorithmic Interest Rates: Compound is a decentralized finance lending platform that offers algorithmically determined interest rates based on supply and demand dynamics for various assets.
- Liquidity Pool Mechanism: Users can supply crypto assets to liquidity pools, earning interest on their deposits while borrowing assets against their holdings.
- Governance Token Model: By holding COMP tokens, users can participate in governance decisions for the future direction of the protocol.

13. Immutable X (IMX)

- Scalable Layer-2 Solution: Immutable X provides a layer-2 scaling solution for Ethereum that allows for fast and secure NFT transactions without gas fees.
- User-Friendly Experience: The platform aims to enhance the user experience by facilitating instant trade confirmations and easy minting of NFTs.
- Partnerships with Major Titles: Immutable X attracts attention through collaborations with leading gaming companies, driving the adoption of its platform.

14. Ondo (ONDO)

- Bridging Traditional and Decentralized Finance: Ondo aims to integrate Real World Assets into the decentralized finance space, providing innovative financial products backed by tangible assets.
- Asset Management Collaborations: By partnering with established asset managers, Ondo offers users credibility and stability in a rapidly evolving landscape.
- Institutional Focus: The platform's focus on institutional-grade products signals a push for mainstream adoption and investor confidence in the decentralized finance ecosystem.

15. Superverse (SUPER)

- Gaming and NFT Integration: Superverse combines immersive gaming experiences with NFT technology, allowing players to trade and own unique digital assets within its ecosystem.
- Play-to-Earn Features: The platform incorporates play-to-earn mechanics, incentivizing engagement and profitability for players.
- Community-Centric Development: By focusing on community input and suggestions, Superverse aims to create an inclusive environment where user interests shape the platform's evolution.

16. Moonwell (WELL)

- Decentralized Lending Protocol: Moonwell facilitates a transparent and user-friendly borrowing and lending experience within the decentralized finance landscape.
- Focus on Community Governance: Emphasizing community governance, Moonwell allows users to influence decisions on protocol changes and future developments.
- Robust Security Audits: The platform prioritizes security, undergoing rigorous audits to build trust and confidence among its user base.

17. Near (NEAR)

- Developer-Friendly Blockchain: NEAR is designed to make decentralized application (dApp) development easy and intuitive, encouraging adoption among developers.
- Scalability Solutions: The platform employs innovative technologies such as sharding to achieve high scalability and low transaction fees.
- Community and Ecosystem: NEAR has fostered a vibrant community and ecosystem, supporting various projects and collaborations that enhance its growth potential.

18. Chainlink (LINK)

- Decentralized Oracle Network: Chainlink connects smart contracts to real-world data, enabling blockchain applications to interact with external data sources.
- Security and Trust: By aggregating data from multiple sources, Chainlink ensures a high level of accuracy and resistance against manipulation.
- Wide Adoption: Many established decentralized finance protocols and projects utilize Chainlink's services, positioning It as a critical infrastructure component in the crypto space.

19. Axelar (AXL)

- Cross-Chain Communication: Axelar facilitates communication between different blockchains, enabling seamless interaction and interoperability.
- Developer Tools: The platform offers tools for developers to build cross-chain applications, promoting wider usage and integration of blockchain solutions.
- Focus on Scalability: Axelar aims to address scalability challenges faced by single-chain networks, enhancing the user experience across multiple ecosystems.

20. Stacks (STX)

- Smart Contracts for Bitcoin: Stacks enables smart contracts to be built directly on Bitcoin, allowing developers to create decentralized applications while leveraging the security and stability of the Bitcoin network.
- Enhanced Functionality: By layering its technology on top of Bitcoin, Stacks introduces features such as programmable money and decentralized finance capabilities, expanding Bitcoin's use cases and functionality.
- Proof of Transfer: Stacks utilizes a unique consensus mechanism called Proof of Transfer (PoX), which connects Stacks to Bitcoin and allows STX holders to earn Bitcoin rewards by participating in the network, incentivizing community engagement, and contributing to Bitcoin's overall ecosystem.

21. Bittensor (TAO)

- Decentralized Neural Network: Bittensor creates a decentralized network that allows participants to contribute computing power and data for training machine learning models, fostering collaboration in artificial intelligence development.
- Incentivized Contributions: Users earn rewards in the form of TAO tokens based on the value their contributions add to the network, encouraging active participation from developers and computing enthusiasts.
- Democratizing Artificial Intelligence: The platform democratizes access to powerful artificial intelligence tools, allowing anyone with computing resources to engage in shaping innovative models and applications.

22. Render (RNDR)

- Decentralized Rendering Services: Render connects digital artists and developers with unused GPU power from other users, providing a decentralized solution for rendering high-quality graphics and animations.
- Cost-Effective Access: By leveraging the network's native RNDR token, users can access rendering services at lower costs compared to traditional centralized providers, making it an attractive option for creatives.
- Impact on Visual Industries: Render's approach facilitates the creation of stunning visuals in gaming, film, and virtual reality, utilizing artificial intelligence to optimize rendering processes and improve quality.

23. Numeraire (NMR)

- Crowdsourced Data Science: Numeraire is integrated with Numerai, a hedge fund that gathers machine learning models from data scientists worldwide, creating a unique ecosystem for predictive analytics in finance.
- Incentivized Predictions: Data scientists can stake Numeraire tokens to submit their predictions, aligning their incentives with the fund's performance and encouraging innovative approaches to investment strategies.
- Influencing Financial Markets: This model fosters a feedback loop where contributors are rewarded based on the accuracy of their models, showcasing the real-world impact of artificial intelligence on financial markets.

24. Fetch.ai (FET)

- Autonomous Agents: Fetch.ai enables the development of autonomous agents capable of performing tasks and interacting with various decentralized applications, enhancing efficiency across multiple industries
- Resource Management: By integrating artificial intelligence and blockchain technology, Fetch.ai optimizes resource management, data sharing, and task automation in sectors such as transportation and logistics.

- Decentralized Ecosystem: The platform supports a diverse array of applications, allowing users to create, manage, and interact with autonomous agents in a decentralized environment, fostering innovation and collaboration.

25. OriginTrail (TRAC)

- Supply Chain Transparency: OriginTrail utilizes blockchain technology and artificial intelligence to enhance transparency and reliability in supply chains, ensuring the traceability of products from source to consumer.
- Decentralized Knowledge Graph: The project's knowledge graph allows for the validation and analysis of supply chain data, helping stakeholders manage and optimize processes while maintaining accountability.
- Improving Business Practices: By providing a decentralized platform for data exchanges, OriginTrail addresses critical challenges in supply chain management, promoting sustainable practices and improving overall efficiency.